My First Book about the Animal Alphabet of the United States

Amazing Animal Books Children's Picture Books

By Molly Davidson

Mendon Cottage Books

JD-Biz Publishing

Read More Amazing Animal Books

Purchase at Amazon.com

Download Free Books!
http://MendonCottageBooks.com

 **is for a Nine-Banded Armadillo.**

The nine-banded armadillo lives in the southern states.

They are nocturnal, which means they look for their food at night; which includes lots of insects, termites, beetles, grasshoppers, and 500 more insects.

 **is for the Bald Eagle.**

The bald eagle lives in Alaska, along the Mississippi River, and in the Rocky Mountains.

The bald eagle is the national bird and animal of the United States; it appears on the official seal.

They build their nests high up on cliffs or in trees so they can easily spot prey.

B  is for an American Bison.

(This "B" is a bonus; we will be skipping the letter "X.")

Bison used to roam all over North America, now they live in protected parks, like Yellowstone National Park and Wood Buffalo National Park.

A bison's think fur is so insulated; snow can land on them without it melting.

The bison is the state animal of Wyoming; it also is on their state flag.

C is for a Crocodile.

Crocodiles live mostly in the swamps of Florida, and the Caribbean area.

A crocodile is different from an alligator because their mouth is a V- shape instead of a U - shape.

Crocodiles can lay up to 60 eggs at one time!

 **is for a White Tailed Deer.**

The white tailed deer live all over the United States in grassy meadows close to forests.

It is the state animal Ohio, South Carolina, Arkansas, and 6 more states.

Only the bucks (boys) grow antlers, which they use to fight for the does (girls) during mating season.

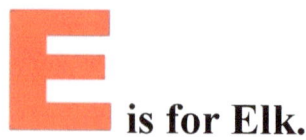 **is for Elk.**

Elk live mostly in the Rocky Mountains.

An elk can grow antlers as long as 4 feet; which they shed every spring and grow back by the fall mating season.

Elk live about 8 to 12 years in the wild.

 **is for a Red Fox.**

The red fox lives in all of North America, all the way up to the Arctic Circle.

A fox's tail helps them keep their balance; they also use it as a warm blanket, and as a flag to talk with other fox.

Fox eat rodents, rabbits, birds, and other small game.

G

is for a Grizzly Bear.

Grizzly bears live in Alaska, Wyoming, Idaho, Washington, and Montana.

Grizzly bears have a very good sense of smell; they can smell food from miles away.

 **is for a Hummingbird.**

Ruby-Throated Hummingbird

The ruby-throated hummingbird lives in the eastern United States, especially along the Mississippi River.

They fly about 30 mph and dive down at speeds of up to 63 mph.

I is for an Indiana Bat.

They live all over the United States, mostly in the Midwest states.

Indiana bats are only 1 to 2 inches long when they are fully grown.

These bats are on the endangered list, due to habitat and food loss.

 **is for a Jaguar.**

Jaguars live in Texas, Arizona, California, and New Mexico; as well as Central and South America.

Jaguars are the largest cats in America; weighing between 100 - 210 pounds.

Jaguars eat deer, crocodiles, turtles, frogs, and fish; basically anything they can catch.

 **is for the last letter in skunK.**

Skunks live all over the United States in burrows or dens.

Skunks will spray a smelly odor ONLY if they feel threatened. They will growl, hiss, stomp, and shake their tails, first, as a warning.

Skunks can eat wasps, honeybees, and poisonous snakes.

L is for a Mountain Lion.

The mountain lion lives in the mountains of the western states.

A mountain lion eats about one deer every week to 10 days.

M is for a Moose.

Moose live in Alaska, New England, New York, the Rocky Mountains, Minnesota, and Michigan.

Moose are the largest members of the deer family; they stand on average 5 to 6 1/2 feet tall.

Moose cannot live where it gets above 80°F, it makes them too sweaty and they may overheat.

 **is for a North American Beaver.**

They live all over the United States and into Canada; the only places they don't live are California and Florida.

The two large front teeth on a beaver never stop growing; they just get filed down when gnawing down trees.

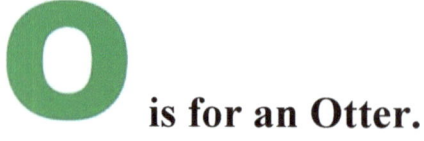 **is for an Otter.**

Otters live in the rivers all over the U.S. except in the deserts and Florida.

River otters can stay under water for up to 8 minutes; they can close their ears and nose to keep the water out.

They like to eat fish, but also shell fish, and frogs.

P

is for a Procyon Lotor (Scientific name for the Northern Raccoon).

The northern raccoon lives from southern Canada through most of the United States down to Mexico.

Raccoon's feet look like human hands, which they use to eat berries, nuts, eggs, shell fish, and insects.

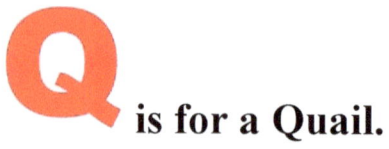 **is for a Quail.**

There are several species of quail; which one species or another can be found all over the United States.

Quails rarely live to be over 1 year old. They have too many predators; like the raccoon, snakes, opossum, hawks, fox, skunk, and humans.

 **is for a Roadrunner.**

Roadrunners live in deserts, grasslands, and woodlands from Missouri to Mexico.

They can run about 20 mph; they can fly but only for short distances.

Roadrunners lay 3 - 6 eggs, and they hatch in about 20 days.

S is for Bighorn Sheep.

Bighorn sheep live mainly the Rocky Mountains and the Sierra Nevada Mountains.

Their horns can be as long as 30 inches and 15 inches wide, they weigh about 30 pounds!

Rams (boys) will compete for the ewes (girls) by head butting; these battles can last up to 24 hours.

T

is for a Texas Longhorn.

They live in the southern part of the United States; and are the mascot for the University of Texas.

Their horns grow straight to the sides of their heads, and can span up to 7 feet.

The longhorn breed registry was established in 1964.

U is for a Utah Prairie Dog.

Utah Prairie dogs live in the grasslands of the central and western United States.

Prairie dogs create habitats for over 150 other species, by their ability to dig huge underground colonies.

V

is for a Vulture (more specifically a California Condor)

The few condors that are left, live in California and Arizona.

The California condor has a wing span of 10 feet, and can fly as high as 3 miles in the air.

They can live up to 60 years in the wild.

W  is for a Gray Wolf.

Wolves live mostly in Alaska and Canada; but some packs live in Montana, Idaho, Minnesota, Wisconsin, Washington, and Michigan.

Every wolf has its own unique howl.

Wolves eat deer, elk, moose, caribou, beavers, rabbits, and will also scavenge for dead animals.

 **is for a Yellow Pine Chipmunk.**

These chipmunks live in the brush covered areas of the western U.S.

They gather and store seeds and nuts all summer and fall, so they will have food to survive through the winter.

Z

Z **is for Zapus Hudsonius (Scientific name for a meadow jumping mouse)**

U.S. Fish and Wildlife Service © <u>Wikimedia Commons</u>

They live from the west coast over to the Great Plains, and as far south as Arizona and Alabama.

Their tails can be as long as 6 1/2 inches.

The babies only need 18 days in their mother before they are born, mice can have up to 9 at one time.

Download Free Books!

http://MendonCottageBooks.com

Our books are available at

1. Amazon.com

2. Barnes and Noble

3. Itunes

4. Kobo

5. Smashwords

6. Google Play Books

Download Free Books!
http://MendonCottageBooks.com

Publisher

JD-Biz Corp

P O Box 374

Mendon, Utah 84325

http://www.jd-biz.com/

www.ingramcontent.com/pod-product-compliance
Lightning Source LLC
Chambersburg PA
CBHW050908290526
45792CB00002B/741